CONTENTS

JUSTIN BIEBER

£7.99

Century
BOOKS

Published 2012. Century Books Ltd.
Unit 1, Upside Station Building Solsbro Road,
Torquay, Devon, UK, TQ26FD

justinbieberstore.com

JUSTIN BIEBER

BACK TO THE BEGINNING

How does a kid from Canada become a global phenomenon with a legion of fans that fill arenas wherever he performs? For Justin Bieber, it's all about the journey...

JB has always displayed a rare and natural talent for music. His ability to turn his hand to a variety of instruments emerged at an early age and he has always been able to sing with real feeling. For the majority of Justin's life, everyone around him has known that he had something special. It was the lessons he learnt growing up however that really set him up for big things.

On March 1st 1994 in London, Ontario, Pattie Mallette and Jeremy Bieber welcomed their first and only child together to the world. Justin had arrived.

Things were tough for Pattie and Jeremy in those early days. The couple were still teenagers and while they both loved and cared deeply for their new baby, the strain on them soon took its toll. When Justin was just ten months old, the pair decided to split up.

Justin and Pattie set up home about an hour away, in a small town called Stratford. Now on her own with a baby to support, Pattie made the move to be nearer to her own parents. Bruce and Diane Dale offered a helping hand looking after Justin while Pattie worked a variety of jobs to make ends meet.

Although life wasn't easy, love was never in short supply. And from watching his mother strive to support them, JB learnt early the value of hard work. Bruce and Diane encouraged Justin in all he did, while Pattie and her friends' love of music quickly rubbed off on the kid. At just four-years-old, Justin showed the first signs that he had a special gift...

"I didn't think of myself as not having a lot of money. But I definitely did not have a lot of money. I couldn't afford to get a lot of new clothes a lot of the time. But I had a roof over my head. I was very fortunate."

"I grew up below the poverty line; I didn't have as much as other people did. I think it made me stronger as a person, it built my character."

"I had my grandparents, I saw them a lot, they were very kind. So I grew up getting everything that I wanted."

JUSTIN BIEBER

JUST THE FACTS JB

Full name:

Justin Drew Bieber

Nicknames:

JB, Biebz, JBiebz or the Kid Rauhl

Date of birth:

1st March 1994

Place on birth:

London, Ontario, Canada

Record label:

Def Jam

Star sign:

Pisces

Height:

5' 7" (1.7m)

Eye colour:

Brown

Languages spoken:

English and French

Instruments played:

Guitar, piano, drums and trumpet

Parents:

Mother Pattie Mallette
Father Jeremy Bieber

Siblings:

Sister Jazmyn, Brother Jaxon

Hidden talent:

"I can solve a Rubik's Cube in under a minute."

Favourite TV show:

Smallville

Favourite food:

Spaghetti Bolognese

Closest friends:

Ryan Butler & Chaz Summers

Likes:

Sports, Tacos & Apple Mac computers

Dislikes:

Ugg boots & Chocolate

Hobbies:

Skateboarding, Ice hockey & Football

Fill this page with pics of all your favourite things!

Jus
Bie

JUST THE FACTS ABOUT YOU!

Here's a special place for you to record all your most essential deets! Fill in these charts with all your info, then add some pics to give a snap shot of your life today.

Name:

Nickname:

Twitter:

Email:

Date of birth:

Star sign:

Height:

Eye colour:

Favourite colour:

Friends:

Family:

Biggest crush:

Top Justin Bieber track:

Other music stars I love:

Favourite website:

Greatest fear:

Top meal:

I've been a Belieber fan for:

I knew I had Bieber fever when:

If I met Justin I would tell him:

The thing I most admire about Justin is:

Believe In JB // Believe In

CRAZY TIMES

On the 23rd April 2012, JB flew into London with a very special package under his arm – eight tracks from the, at the time, unreleased album 'Believe'!

From the moment he touched down at Heathrow Airport, Justin's whistle stop trip to the capital was out of control! Hundreds of fans had turned up to meet him as he made his way through customs, while even more were waiting outside his hotel.

The five star Royal Garden Hotel in Kensington was besieged by fans, literally. Security had to help Justin and his team safely inside, but the insania didn't stop there. The Sun newspaper reported that they had received more than 2,000 calls a day from Beliebers asking to be put through to JB's room during his short stay. Justin even had to wear a disguise to slip out in the evening to visit a local McDonalds for a McFlurry!

TWEET: "Wow. Airport was crazy getting to London! All worth it for my Beliebers. Some people always tryna ruin it for the fans. Not today Swaggy"

IN THE CAPITAL

The craziness followed the star everywhere he went, including work. With tweets flying around all the time JB was in town, the icon was never off of Twitter's trending charts. During an interview with Capital FM to reveal he would perform at the station's Summertime Ball, he was even forced to explain who Jerry was! Confused? Check out the interview yourself on YouTube. As JB revealed, sometimes his fans are inappropriate, but that's just another reason why he loves them!

TWEET:
"Eating a steak and gonna get a good night's rest and relax. I hear u guys outside the hotel... and I LOVE U!"

TWEET:
"This girl sat on the hood of my car today in London. She was like, He isn't going anywhere..."

TWEET:
"Chillin with @JeremyBieber in the UK. Swaggy"

ve In JB //Believe In JB //Believe In JB //Believe In JB //Believe In JB //Believe In JB //Believe In JB //Believe In JB
JB //Believe In JB //Believe In JB //Believe In JB //Believe In JB //Believe In JB //Believe In JB //Believe In JB

13

Believe In JB //Believe In JB //Believe In JB //Believe In JB //Believe In JB //Believe In JB //Believe In JB //Believe In JB //Believe In JB //Believe In JB //Believe
In JB //Believe In JB //Believe In JB //Believe In JB //Believe In JB //Believe In JB //Believe In JB //Believe In JB //Believe In JB //Believe In JB //
Believe In JB // Believe In JB //Believe In JB //Believe In JB //Believe In JB //Believe In JB //Believe In JB //Believe In JB //Believe In JB //Believe In JB //Believe In JB //Believe

SOMETHING TO GET

Justin wasn't in London just to catch up, he also had some serious business to attend to. Several hundred of the world's most important and respected music journalists were invited to an exclusive event at Supperclub in West London's Notting Hill.

At the event, Justin was interviewed by Radio One's Reggie Yates. The star gave his thoughts on his new album and let people hear, for the first time, his new more mature sounds. No one was disappointed.

TWEET:
"Being on promo feels really good. Glad to be back working and seeing the fans. WE STILL GOT IT. My fans go HARD!"

TWEET:
"Great listening session today with international press in Notting Hill. Good to finally let people hear some of #BELIEVE"

EXCITED ABOUT

elieve' shows JB as he is now – older, wiser and more experienced. The press were blown away by how Justin's ong-writing had grown, how his voice had matured nd the incredible producers and collaborators who had orked with JB on the record. Reviews were glowing cross the board.

ith his previous albums and tour, Justin had already roved he was a one of a kind teen star. After just one play 'Believe', JB proved that he had the style and substance o be a major force in the music industry now and for years o come.

TWEET: "Actually happy to be back out doing promo. Missed seeing everyone. Good day of interviews today. Just want #BELIEVE to get here already."

TWEET: "Interviews this morning. Think it went well. Want to say THANK YOU to all the UK fans who showed love these last few days"

TWEET: "Who am I? the luckiest guy on the planet. I fight for what I believe in but I have millions next to me. Thank you. #BestFansEVER"

YOUR ULTIMATE JB PLAYLIST!

The great thing about music, especially JB's, is that no matter what your mood is like, there's always the perfect track out there to accompany it. On dark days it can lift you up, it can take you right back to a special memory or turn a party into a major event!

Sometimes finding a tight tune at the right time can be hard. It pays to get yourself organized! Fill in these handy playlists, programme them into your MP3 or phone and the next time you're in urgent need of the perfect tune, you'll have a playlist ready and waiting to go!

My just Justin playlist:

00:00 00:00

Track: ....

Track: ....

Track: ....

Track: ....

Track: ....

My chill down playlist:

00:00 00:00

Artist: ....
Track: ....

Artist: ....
Track: ....

Artist: ....
Track: ....

Artist: ....
Track: ....

Artist: ....
Track: ....

My swag party playlist:

Artist: ....
Track: ....

Artist: ....
Track: ....

Artist: ....
Track: ....

Artist: ....
Track: ....

Artist: ....
Track: ....

Artist: ....
Track: ....

Artist: ....
Track: ....

Artist: ....
Track: ....

Artist: ....
Track: ....

My party rock playlist

Artist: ....
Track: ....

Artist: ....
Track: ....

Artist: ....
Track: ....

Artist: ....
Track: ....

Artist: ....
Track: ....

Artist: ....
Track: ....

Artist: ....
Track: ....

Artist: ....
Track: ....

Artist: ....
Track: ....

STRICTLY

It doesn't matter whether you're singing along with a hairbrush in your room, hollering with your people at school or humming to JB tunes with your iPod on – you can't get enough of Justin's music, right?

When you get down to JB, are you word perfect or mumbled mess-up? More importantly, are you catching the meaning behind each memorable melody? Now's the time to find out. Grab a pen, study each Bieber lyric and fill in the missing words.

1 Boyfriend: Tell me what you like yeah, tell me what you don't, I could be your _ _ _ _ _ _ _ _ _ _ _ _ fly you across the globe...

2 Eenie Meenie: You seem the type to love them and leave them, And disappear right _ _ _ _ _ _ _ _ _ _ _ _ _ _...

3 You're my special little lady: The one _ _ _ _ _ _ _ _ _ _ _ _ crazy...

4 Baby: Are we an item? Girl, quit playing, ' _ _ _ _ _ _ _ _ _ _ _ _ _ _ _ _, what are you saying?

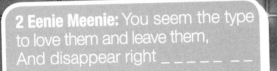

5 One Time: When I met you girl my heart went knock knock, Now them _ won't stop stop...

6 One Less Lonely Girl: How many I told yous, And _ _ _ _ _ _ _ _ _ _ and shoulders...

7 Somebody To Love: For you I'd write a symphony, I'd tell the violin it's _ _ _ _ _ _ _ _ _ _ _ _ _ _ _...

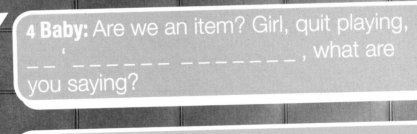

8 U Smile: If you need me I'll come running, From a _ _ _ _ _ _ _ _ _ _ _ _ _ _ away...

LYRICS »

9 Pray: I lose my appetite, knowing kids starve tonight, Am I a sinner, cos __ __ _____ still there on the plate?

10 Never Say Never: I'm strong enough to climb the highest tower, And I'm fast enough __ __ ___ _____ ___ ___-...

11 Mistletoe: Word on the street Santa's coming tonight, _____ _____ in the sky so high...

12 Love Me: My friends say I'm a fool to think you're the one for me, I guess I'm just a _____ ___ ___-...

13 From Never Let You Go: Let the music blast, we gonna do our dance, Bring the _____ __ they don't matter at all...

14 First Dance: When I close my eyes I see me and you at the prom, We've been both _____ __ _ ___ for this day to come...

15 Common Denominator: When broken hearts rise up to say 'love is a lie',You and I ____ _____ to be love's reply yeah...

16 Believe: There were nights when I doubted myself, But you ____ __ _____ from falling, Look at us now...

17 All Around The World: DJ bring that back, All around the world, I want __ __ _____-...

18 Die In Your Arms: Every time you touch me it just feels so right, So ____ ____ ___ please don't stop girl...

19 As long as you love me: We could be starving, We could __ _____,

20 Why should we: _____ ___ _____, Cause I'm in love with the thought of you...

JUSTIN BIEBER

GROWING UP BIEBER

Before Justin even started school, he was already picking out songs on the drums, guitar and piano. Pattie and her friends could see JB had a natural talent for music but it would be a few years before he would be ready to go professional!

Justin attended the Jeanne Sauve Catholic school in Stratford, a French language speaking school, and quickly settled in. As well as music, JB also had a love of sports and enrolled in many clubs. He played football and also joined an after-school ice hockey club. It was at hockey that Justin met two friends who remain his best buddies to this day – Chaz Somers and Ryan Butler.

When not hanging out with Ryan and Chaz, Justin was home using the hard work ethic he inherited from his mother Pattie to learn about music. JB practiced religiously, taking much inspiration from the great artists he heard on the radio. Pattie and her friends turned Justin on to a variety of different sounds and although he didn't live with his dad Jeremy, JB's father was also a big part of his life. Whenever the two got together Jeremy would play Justin all his favourite rock songs.

JB was making music purely for the love of it and, with all the practice, he improved quickly. The youngster soon felt ready to take his passion to the next level. A young Justin was full of ambition, but even he would have been surprised if he'd known then that by the tender age of 12, his talents would be shared with the whole world!

"I have a great relationship with my dad. When I was younger, he taught me how to play some songs on the guitar, like 'Knockin' on Heaven's Door' by Bob Dylan."

"Although I might not agree with her all the time, she's [JB's mum] always right. She taught me everything."

"Dad's the one who got me into classic rock and then turned me on to stuff like Guns N' Roses and Metallica. He's cool."

BEHIND THE TRACKS

BELIEVE

Even though JB's new album was shrouded in secrecy, Justin revealed some key details on Twitter during his time in the recording studio. After two ultra successful albums, over a year spent touring the world, appearances on the big and small screens and turning eighteen, 'Believe' introduces us to an altogether more grown up, cool and worldly-wise JB. Let's take a look at some of the key tracks…

Track: Boyfriend

The first taste of Justin's new sound, 'Boyfriend' became an instant classic as soon as it was released. Featuring breathy rapping and Justin's strong falsetto voice, it left no one in any doubt that a new JB had arrived.

JB worked on the track with Mike Posner, famous for the song 'Cooler Than Me', and respected producer Mason Levy. 'Boyfriend's hip-hop and R&B sound was a hit with fans and critics.

Track: Die In Your Arms

After his previous successes, the biggest names in music now line up to work with JB. Super-producer Rodney Jerkins, known as Dark Child, has been at the helm for some of the biggest songs by artists including Beyoncé and Michael Jackson. Now he is eager to sprinkle some of his magic on a JB joint!

The two team up on the track 'Die In Your Arms', a slick R&B song about love and meeting the girl of your dreams.

Track: All Around The World

When JB flew into London to play tracks off 'Believe' for the first time, 'All Around The World' immediately stood out. The electronic, dancefloor-filling, club banger sees Justin teaming up with Ludacris for the first time since 'Baby', but the tracks couldn't be further apart. If you want to party, put this on and turn the volume up!

Track: Believe

Justin's relationship with his fans is one of the most important in his life. So during the making of his album, writing and dedicating a song to Beliebers was a number one priority.

"This is a track I wrote for my fans and is about how they inspired me. Listen to the words... It means a lot. I wrote it on my birthday – it was midnight in the studio and Scooter wanted to sing happy birthday to me but I was like 'no, let me finish this song!'"

The song is a gospel-tinged epic – the perfect way for Justin to say 'thank you'.

Track: Be Alright

Although he now has access to the greatest producers, musicians and studios in the world, on 'Be Alright' Justin shows he can still handle things on his own when he needs to. Written on a plane to Indonesia, JB recorded the track with just a guitar for accompaniment when he landed on the island. He describes the song itself as "a mix between Fergie and Jesus."

Track: Right Here

As well as hooking up with established producers, Justin was also keen to work with hot new talent. 'Hit Boy' has worked with Lil' Wayne and Eminem but came to wider attention when he worked with JB and Drake on 'Believe'. Swagger, R&B and hip-hop make it a track you can't help but bounce along to. It's sure to be a live favourite for years to come.

Track: Thought Of You

One of JB's favourites on the album, 'Thought Of You' sees the artist teaming up with Diplo. The producer made his name working with artists like M.I.A, Nicola Roberts and as a member of Major Lazer he brings all of his individual style to the track.

'Thought Of You' is another electro-dance smash that shows that Justin is equally at home now on stage or in a club!

Track: As Long As You Love Me

If one track from Believe can really sum up Justin's new sound, this is it. Bass heavy and packed with hand claps, it's impossible not to tap your feet to it. Justin worked with Rodney Jerkins again on this track and it's clear the pair are a match made in musical heaven. At his album listening event in London, JB admitted he loves it, remarking, "Man, this is a really good song!" We couldn't agree more.

JUSTIN BIEBER

A-Z

Know all there is to know about JB? Time to get back in class!

A is for… 'All I Want For Christmas Is You'
JB's duet with Mariah Carey was a Christmas hit all around the world. The pair had a ball filming the song's video in Macy's – New York's world famous department store.

B is for… 'Believe'
Now an 18-year-old, JB's latest album shows a more developed, grown-up sound for Justin. It also features a host of his favourite artists.

C is for… Canada
Even though he now lives in Atlanta in the US, Justin is fiercely loyal to his Canadian roots. He calls the country, the "greatest in the world."

D is for… Dancing
Justin can hold his own on stage with some of the world's best dancers, none more impressive than mentor Usher. JB proved just how much he loves to dance when on stage with LMFAO IN 2011.

E is for… Extended Play
At just seven tracks, JB's first collection of songs wasn't long enough to be deemed a full album so 'My World' was classified as an EP.

F is for… French
After attending Jean Sauve in Stratford, a French immersion school, Justin has become fluent in French.

G is for… Gomez
Justin and, former Wizards Of Waverly Place star, Selena, have been an item for over two years. They stepped out together in public for the first time at the 2011 Oscars®.

H is for… Haircut
When Justin had his famous swish hairstyle trimmed to a cool crop it was called the "most expensive haircut of all time" as a lock of Justin's hair reportedly sold for over £25,000 and went to charity.

I is for… International
Justin was born in Canada, taught in French, lives in America and tours the world. JB's global baby!

J is for… Jon Chu
Justin worked with the director of Step Up 2: The Streets on the box office smash hit film Justin Bieber – Never Say Never 3D.

K is for… Kingston
One of JB's best friends is Sean Kingston. The pair collaborated together on the track 'Eenie Meenie', hit each other up on Twitter and hang out as much as their busy schedules allow.

L is for… Los Angeles
During the 'My World' tour, JB performed in the city's huge Staples Center venue. Justin relived the famous scene from the Adam Sandler movie Mr Deeds and booked the whole arena for a romantic candlelit dinner with Selena Gomez.

M is for… My World 2.0
Justin's first full-length studio album was released in March 2010. It took JB to the top of the charts all around the world.

N is for... Ne-Yo
Justin received hundreds of thousands of hits on YouTube after his mum Pattie posted a video of him performing the R&B's star classic hit 'So Sick'. Check it out, you won't regret it.

O is for... One Time
Justin's first single was a huge smash when it was released in 2009. Music industry big wigs were quick to mark JB out as major new force in music – he hasn't let them down.

P is for... Punk'd
JB is a huge practical joker so he jumped at the chance to appear on the MTV show. He managed pull tricks on Taylor Swift, Miley Cyrus and Sean Kingston, although Rob Dydrek saw through JB's ruse.

Q is for... Quick!
Tickets to his 'My World tour' sold out in Twenty-two minutes for every single seat at Madison Square Garden, while all seven nights of his Australian tour went in under fifteen minutes!

R is for... the Raymond Braun Media Group
Scooter and Usher's company signed Justin in 2008 after quickly recognising his potential to become a global superstar.

S is for... Stratford
The small town in Ontario, Canada that JB calls home. When he's not out on the road, Justin can often be found here hanging out with his homies.

T is for... Twitter
JB is a major tweeter! His number of followers is growing daily – at the last count he had over 20million. Are you one? If not, head over to Twitter.com and join the family @justinbieber.

U is for... Under The Mistletoe
With his 2011 Christmas themed album, Justin proved that holiday albums can be cool!

V is for... Venezuela
Justin finished his 'My World' tour by performing for 14,000 people in Caracas, Venezuela's capital city on 19th October 2011.

W is for... We Are The World 25 for Haiti.
JB showed his caring side when joined a who's who of music stars on this single for the Haiti earthquake relief charity.

X is for... X Factor
No doubt Justin has it in abundance! He's also one of the few artists to have appeared on both the UK and US version of the show. He even recently said he could see himself being a judge in the future.

Y is for... YouTube
JB hits more than 1.5million subscribers every time he posts a video online to his YouTube channel. Going by the name 'Kid Rauhl' JB's Youtube videos have been viewed 2.8 billion times making him the most viewed artist ever!

Z is for... Jay-Z
Justin caused a sensation on Twitter when he tweeted a picture of himself hanging out with mega-rapper Jay-Z, Kanye West, and host of cool music stars in December 2011.

THE COLLABORATION KING

Although he's a solo artist, JB understands the power of teamwork. Throughout his career he's jumped at the chance to work with some of the biggest names in industry. The results speak for themselves! Meet just a few of the top tier talent that Justin's made music with.

Usher

As well as being Justin's mentor and part of his management team, Usher has also lent his voice to JB's tunes. The pair hooked up for 'The Christmas Song (Chestnuts Roasting On An Open Fire)' from JB's 'Under The Mistletoe' album. The pair's vocals proved the perfect blend. Expect them to team up again soon!

Ludacris

As well as basing himself in Atlanta, Justin has also thrown himself into the city's music scene. So when he was looking for a rapper to sprinkle some flavour on the track 'Baby', Justin called in Ludacris, the town's finest rapper. Usher and Luda had teamed up previously on the global smash 'Yeah!' so JB knew his track was in good hands!

Rascal Flatts

Being a guitarist himself, Justin's always had soft spot for country music. He was totally over-excited to work with country super stars Rascal Flatts on the track That Should Be Me'. The ensuring recording became an overwhelming crossover success and even won JB a Country Music Television award for 'Collaboration Of The Year'.

Mariah Carey

Justin fulfilled a personal dream when he got to work wit superstar singer Mariah Carey. The pair duetted on a new version of Mariah's 1993 classic 'All I Want For Christma Is You' – the track went on to be yet another global smas

Sean Kingston

Justin hooked up his good friend Sean to create a special track for his first album. 'Eenie Meenie' is a cool R&B summer pop tune that helped establish both JB and Sean in the charts after its release in 2010.

Far East Movement

As well as having celebrity friends and musical inspirations on his own albums, Justin also loves to appear on other artist's records. JB seized the chance to lay some vocals on dance pop band Far East Movement's track 'Live My Life'. The track blew up in the clubs and introduced a whole new crowd to Bieber!

Jaden Smith

Justin and Jade worked together on 'Never Say Never' and the results were so good it was used as the title song for JB's first film and also the main theme tune for Jaden's movie The Karate Kid.

Miley Cyrus

Hannah Montana star Miley, a good friend of Justin's girlfriend Selena Gomez, appeared with JB on a live version of the song 'Overboard'. Lucky fans at Justin's sell out Madison Square Garden show in August 2010 got a treat when Miley joined Justin live on stage.

Kanye West

Megastar rapper Kanye gave Justin's track 'Runaway Love' the West treatment when he remixed it for Justin's album 'Never Say Never: The Remixes'. The pals both tweeted about how happy they were with the results, promising to work together again soon.

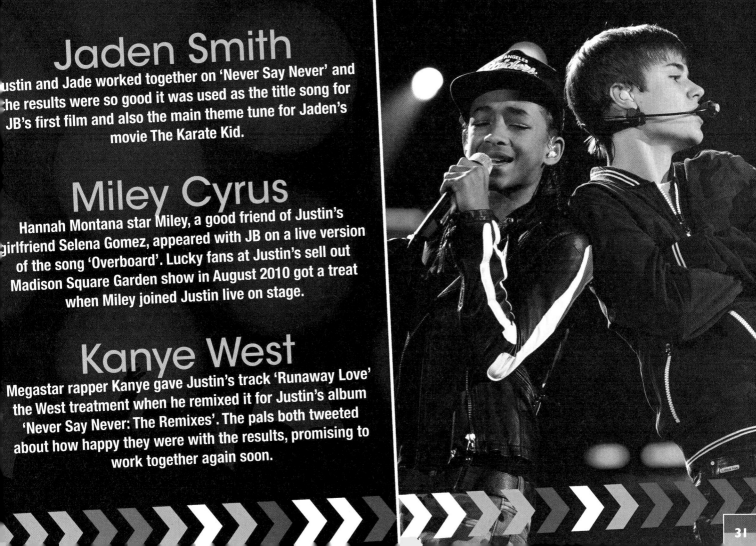

TRICKY

It's one thing knowing the words to a few of Justin's mega hits, but you can't call yourself a true Belieber unless you know 'em all! We've gathered up some lyrics from some of JB's lesser-known (but equally amazing!) music. Can you write the song titles that these snippets of lyrics come from?

If the going gets tough, turn to the answers on page 92…

1. .... See like Adam and Eve, tragedy was a destiny, Like Sonny and Cher, baby I don't care, I got you baby, _ _ _ _ _ _ _ _ _ _ _ _ _ _ _

2. .... So crazy is this we call love, And now that we've got it we just can't give it up, _ _ _ _ _ _ _ _ _

3. .... We'll take it to the sky, pass the moon to the galaxy, As long as you're with me, baby, honestly, _ _

4. .... You said you needed a little time for my mistakes, It's funny how you used that time to have me replaced, _ _ _ _ _ _ _ _ _ _ _ _

5. .... Mommy, you were always and somewhere, And Daddy, I live out of town, So tell me, how could I ever be normal somehow? _ _ _ _ _ _ _ _ _ _

6. .... The DJ's playing my favourite song, ain't no chaperons, This could be the night of your dreams, _ _ _ _ _ _ _ _ _

7. .... And all the haters, I swear they look so small from up here,

8. .... I'm gonna live my life No matter what, we party tonight _ _ _ _ _ _ _ _

TITLES ≫

9. .... I feel the chemistry, With everything we make, A little kiss is a definite possibility, _ _ _ _ _ _ _ _ _ _ _

10. .... This life can kick you around, This world can make you feel small, _ _ _ _ _ _ _ _ _ _ _ _ _ _ _ _ _

11. .... Yeah, she's got cash, Pocket so thick she don't even have to ask, _ _ _ _ _ _ _ _

12. .... When you open your eyes, When the lights go bright girl, I'll be right there, _ _ _ _ _ _

13. .... Yeah, you are my dream, There's not a thing I won't do, I'll give up my life for you, Cos you are my dream, _ _ _ _ _ _ _ _

14. .... Pacing down the hallway, Trying to fight the urge to call, I could almost hear a pin drop, _ _ _ _ _ _ _ _ _ _ _ _ _ _ _ _

15. .... And I'm sorry if I pushed you away, I just want you to know I miss you, And I want you to stay, _ _ _ _ _ _ _ _ _ _ _ _

16. .... You're beautiful, you should know it, You're crazy girl, you should know it, _ _ _ _ _ _ _ _ _ _ _ _ _ _

17. .... I could just die in your arms, Every time you touch me it just feels so right, _ _ _ _ _ _ _ _ _ _ _ _

18. .... We could be starving, we could be homeless, we could be broke, I'll be your platinum, I'll be your silver, I'll be your gold, _ _ _ _ _ _ _ _ _

19. .... Gonna take some time but I'll figure it out, Why should we fight the feeling, _ _ _ _ _ _ _ _ _ _

20. .... All alone in my room, waiting for your call, For you I'd walk a thousand miles, Through the long nights and bright lights, _ _ _ _ _ _ _ _ _

A BIG HAND FOR...
JUSTIN BIEBER

Justin Bieber

JB is an awards machine! Since exploding on to the scene in 2009 he's been nominated for a host of top industry gongs, walking away with more than 55 major honours. We just hope his house in Atlanta is big enough to fit them all in! Here's a big handful of the musical accolades he's won so far…

2010

American Music Awards
- Artist of the Year
- Favourite Pop/Rock Male Artist
- T-Mobile Breakthrough Artist
- Favourite Pop/Rock album

MTV Brazil Music Awards
- International Artist

MTV Europe Music Awards
- Best Male
- Best Push Act

MTV Video Music Awards
- Best New Artist

Much Music Awards
- UR Fave: New Artist
- UR Fave: Canadian Video: 'Baby'

Myx Music Awards
- Favourite International Video: 'One Time'

Teen Choice Awards
- Male Artist
- Breakout Artist: Male
- Choice Summer Music Star: Male
- Choice Music Pop Album

TRL Awards
- Best International Act
- Young Hollywood Awards
- Newcomer Of The Year

2011

BRIT Awards
- International Breakthrough Artist

Juno Awards
- Fan Choice Award
- Pop Album Of The Year

Nickelodeon Kid's Choice
- Favourite Male Singer
- Favourite Song: 'Baby'

Billboard Music Awards
- Top New Artist
- Top Social Artist
- Top Streaming Artist
- Top Digital Media Artist
- Top Pop Album
- Top Streaming Song: 'Baby'

CMT Awards
- Collaborative Video of the Year:
  'That Should Be Me' feat. Rascal Flatts

MTV Movie Awards
- Best Jaw-dropping Moment:
  Justin Bieber – Never Say Never 3D

2012

NRJ Awards
- NRJ Award Of Honour

Nickelodeon Kid's Choice Awards
- Favourite Male Singer

JUSTIN BIEBER

WORKING HARD

Justin made his first steps towards fame and fortune when he was just 12 years old. In January 2007, he entered a local talent show called the Stratford Star. Up against a variety of acts, if he came first, Justin would have won a new microphone, but the prize was not important – JB really wanted to know if everything he had been working on at home would connect with a real audience.

Justin sang three songs, Matchbox 20's '3AM', Alicia Keys' 'Fallin'' and Aretha Franklin's classic 'Respect'. The youngster was knocked out when he won a very respectable third place in the competition. Pattie, bursting with pride, recorded JB's performances and posted them onto YouTube. The videos became the first of many online. Each time, Justin and Pattie were surprised by the instant interest the footage attracted. The pair started having fun recording more videos of Justin singing hits and putting them on the web. As the views increased, so Justin's talent grew.

Justin's performance at the Stratford Star taught him that he needed to work on singing in front of an audience. Getting gigs can be tough when you're so young – the normal places aspiring musicians perform, such as bars and clubs, are off limits to anyone under age. Justin decided to take his talent to the streets instead. Every weekend he'd take his guitar into town and sit on the steps of the Stratford Theatre.

Justin's hard work paid off. His busking soon proved a hit with the people of Stratford, but it was his YouTube videos that were to make the real difference. Now music industry movers and shakers were starting to pay attention…

"He was doing something different. He was an attractive white kid singing very soulful R&B hits. That set him apart immediately from anyone in his range because no one was covering or singing these kind of records. But equally important was that you believe in these songs 😊 it was real. And you wanted to hear more."

Chris Hicks, A&R Island/Def Jam

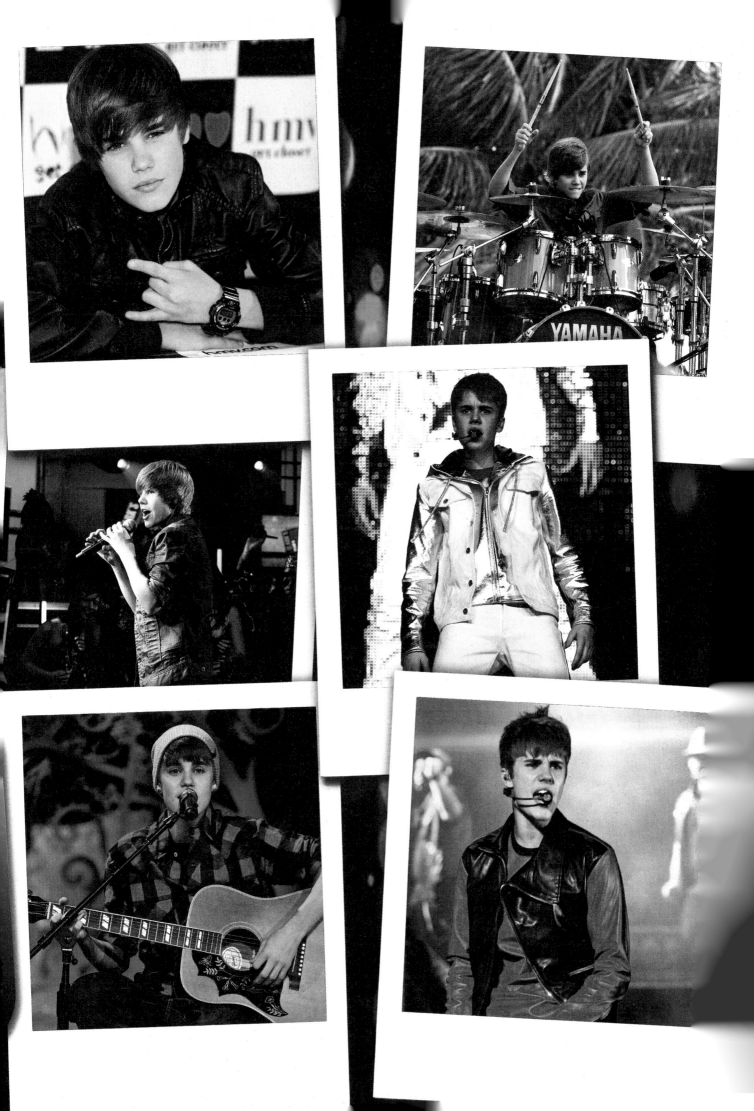

JUSTIN BIE

Justin likes 21 different pages from his own Facebook page. Just three belong to fellow musicians (Usher, Asher Roth and Taylor Swift), one is a TV show (The Today Show) while the other 17 are all charities.

In just one day, the teaser video for Justin's 'Boyfriend' video received 65,163 likes on Facebook.

Justin's own YouTube channel is run under the name Kid Rauhl. He took the name from his father Jeremy who is a big fan of author Terry Goodkind's Sword of Truth books, which include a character called Lord Rauhl.

Back in November, JB narrowly beat Lady Gaga to become the first artist to clock up 1billion views on YouTube.

Since joining Twitter in 2009, Justin has been gaining an average 24,000 new followers everyday. He currently has over 22million!

LETS GET

SOCIA

How big is Justin on Twitter? Well, in 2010 Twitter themselves reported that 83% of everyone who uses their site are Justin Bieber fans!

But it's not always plain sailing for JB on Twitter. When he cut off his famous 'swish' hairstyle in January 2011, Justin lost 80,000 followers overnight!

Justin, as Kid Rauhl, has posted 82 videos to his YouTube channel, which have been viewed over 393million times so far!

Justin's first video on YouTube was a cover of Chris Brown's 'With You' recorded at his home in Stratford when he was just 13 years old.

Justin has more than 43million Facebook likes!

JB loves to follow his fans back on Twitter. At the last count he was following 123,057 people.

Justin is a huge fan of the iPod game Temple Run, often posts screengrabs of his best scores on his Instagram page. Fancy taking on JB and beating his PB? You'll need some practice – his top score currently is an awesome 9,290,772.

JB is one of the most interactive stars in the world. The star can alwa found online chatting to fans, giving followers a look behind the sce his life and posting whatever is on his mind! Since bursting onto t in 2009, Justin has set a bunch of records with his Twitter, YouT Facebook and Instagram pages. It's a crazy online life!

Discover what Justin Bieber's upto right now, anywhere

About me | Family | Tour | Studio | Whats next? | Hobbies

You don't get more than 20million followers on Twitter if you can't write a good tweet! Justin has put his 140 character updates to brilliant use since he joined the Internet phenomenon in March 2009. Since then he's tweeted more than 14,000 times – here are ten of his best.

'It's about that time… RANDOM CHUCK NORRIS MOMENT: #ChuckNorris does not style his hair, it lays perfectly in place out of sheer fear!' **Twitter gives fans an uncensored look into what is on Justin's mind at any time of the day. Perhaps a little censoring might be good!**

'@ConanOBrien congrats on the new show… curse you for your incredible charm and stylish hair that puts my mop to shame!' **One JB's many tweets about his famous hair!**

'It's funny when I read things about myself that are just not true. Why would certain people take time out of their day to hate on a 16-year-old?' **For the most part, Justin uses his Twitter to have fun, but occasionally he'll let people know what's bothering him too.**

'I haven't shaved my head in a long time, feels kinda cool. I used to shave it every summer. All good. It grows back. Anyway…' Ever the pranker, Biebz tricked his fans into believing he'd shaved all of his hair off on April Fools Day.

'I'm about my fans. I don't let the down. I don't leave them. I'm there for them the way they r there for me. #FAMILY' Biebz frequently tells his fans how much they mean to him.

'#BLESSED to have the #GREATESTFANSON THEPLANET - #GRATEFUL to #LOVEthe BELIEBERS – 19million sexy *#$%@#%@% - haha!' **You can tell Justin was pretty pleased to get past the 19million followers mark!**

'#24HOURS It can finally not be the hype about the rumours, or the business, or where or what happened. It can finally be back to the MUSIC!' **JB joined fans as they counted down to the release of his comeback single 'Boyfriend' and revealed he couldn't be happier to be getting new music out there.**

'A lot of doubt lately. What will I do? What will it sound like? Is he over? Is he fading? But U all never stopped BELIEVING in me. THANK U' **Justin was relieved when 'Boyfriend' received such a good reception, sharing his victory with the fans.**

'Yo @itunesmusic I'm trying to romance 19million ladies with my music. You are kinda screwing this up for me. Leggo!' **'Boyfriend' was soon topping download charts but it wasn't all plain-sailing – Biebz tweeted iTunes to moan about the delay in them recording their figures!**

'I give up a personal life, I give up friends and family to pursue what I love and make fans happy.' **JB drops a quote from an interview with Complex magazine to explain his choices.**

STEP UP TO... THE 2013 BIEBER QUIZ

OK, here's another chance to give your JB knowledge a total workout! Taking part couldn't be simpler – all you have to do is grab a pen and answer as many questions as you can.

When you've finished up, turn to page 92 and mark your efforts (no flicking ahead and cheating mind!). Now you're ready to total up your score and find out what your JB level is!

What was Justin's huge world tour called?

Write down the title of JB's first single.

What are the names of Justin's younger brother and sister?

JBiebz plays guitar, drums, piano and what other instrument?

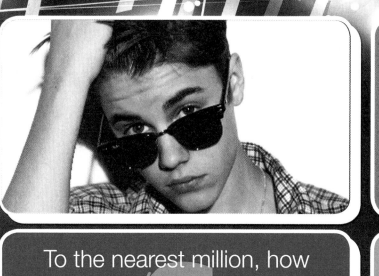

In which month does Justin celebrate his birthday?

To the nearest million, how many followers does Justin have on Twitter?

When out on the road, Justin has a nickname for the entourage who travel everywhere with him. What are they called?

How many tattoos does Justin have?

Justin performed his first showcase for music industry big wigs in Atlanta, Georgia. Can you name the venue?

Which rapper and actor appeared with Justin on his biggest hit to date, 'Baby'?

Jaden Smith featured on the track 'Never Say Never' with JB. Justin also took another member of the Smith clan with him on tour, who was it?

Before hitting the big time, Justin honed his skills recording YouTube videos. How else did he work on his music?

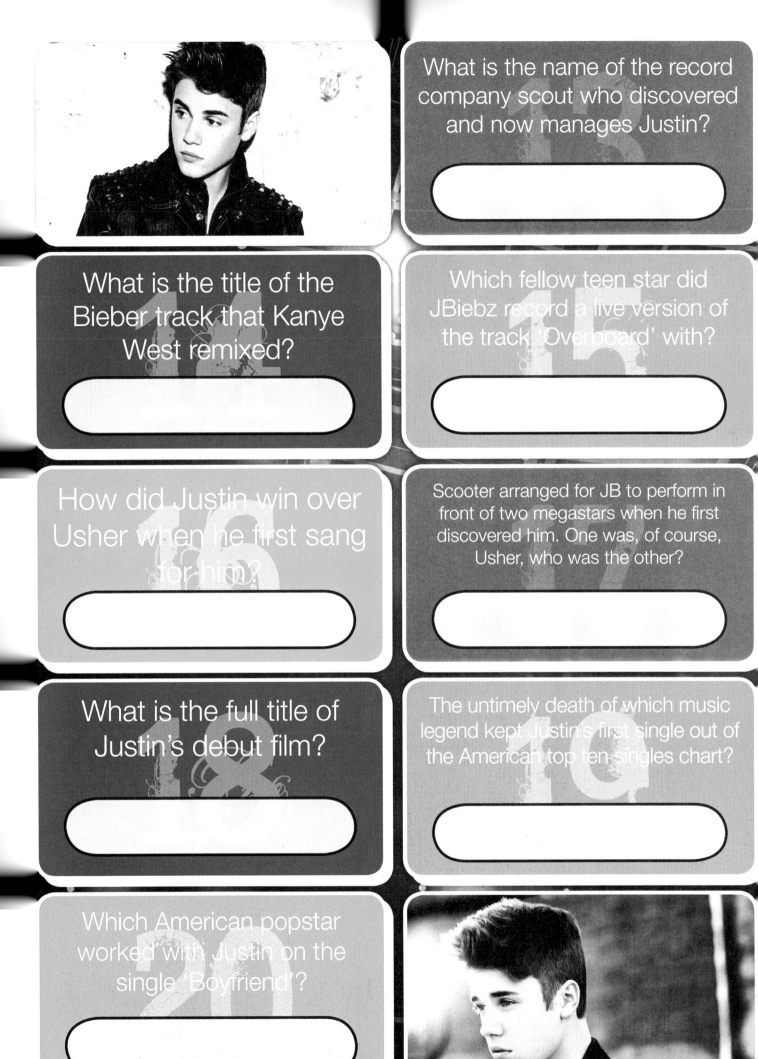

What is the name of the record company scout who discovered and now manages Justin?

What is the title of the Bieber track that Kanye West remixed?

Which fellow teen star did JBiebz record a live version of the track 'Overboard' with?

How did Justin win over Usher when he first sang for him?

Scooter arranged for JB to perform in front of two megastars when he first discovered him. One was, of course, Usher, who was the other?

What is the full title of Justin's debut film?

The untimely death of which music legend kept Justin's first single out of the American top ten singles chart?

Which American popstar worked with Justin on the single 'Boyfriend'?

What is the name of the record company scout who discovered and now manages Justin?

Who did JB team up with on 'The Christmas Song – Chestnuts Roasting On An Open Fire?'

How old was Justin when he got his first drum kit?

In which small town did Justin shoot the video to 'One Less Lonely Girl?'

Justin's maternal grandparents have a big influence on his life. What are their names?

STEP UP TO... THE **2013** BIEBER QUIZ HOW DID YOU DO?

0-15

You are an entry level Belieber, but don't feel downhearted, the only way is up. With a little swotting you'll soon have raised your JB knowledge to swag level!

16-20

Your knowledge of Justin is incredible, but there is always room for improvement! We prescribe you two or three reads of this very annual to whip your Bieber brain into shape.

21-25

Wow! Are you Justin in disguise?! You are a level three, third degree, triple dan, top-of-the-tree Belieber. Keep up the good work, you totally rock!

JUSTIN BIEBER

Justin Bieber

YOU & YOURS

With his family, friends, fans and a speed dial brimming with musical collaborators, there's a lot of people that make up JB's crew. Who's who in yours? Get your camera out, take some snaps of your family and friends, then stick them in here.

ME AND MY BEST MATES

CHILLING WITH THE FAM

MY BELIEBER CREW

HANGING WITH THE SCHOOL POSSE

Printer out of ink? Camera out of battery? Don't despair! Find some felt-tipped pens and fill the frames with the portraits of all the people that matter.

JUSTIN BIEBER

Justin Bieber

JUSTIN BIEBER

53

CAMERA BELIEVE!

JB is confirmed genius behind the microphone, but he's also proving himself something of a phenomenon in front of the camera too. Whether he's appearing on a talk show, guest mentoring on a TV talent show, acting in a drama or appearing in his own documentary – Justin is ever cool, calm and confident. Take a look through some of the stars on screen highlights. How many did you catch?

This Is Justin Bieber

This Is Justin Bieber aired on ITV 10th December 2011 and saw the teenage star take to the stage to perform these well-known hits, *Mistletoe, Never Say Never, Pray, Santa Claus Is Coming To Town, Drummer Boy, You Got It Bad, Because of You, Christmas Love* and *Baby* as well as footage of Bieber visiting different parts of the UK. The hour-long programme, which was presented by Reggie Yates and showed the story behind Justin's rise to fame.

Late Night with David Letterman

An interview with comedian and talk show legend Dave Letterman can be a nerve-wracking experience for any celebrity, but not Justin! JB has appeared on Letterman's show several times and held his own with the quick-witted host, even when having to deal with some tricky lines of

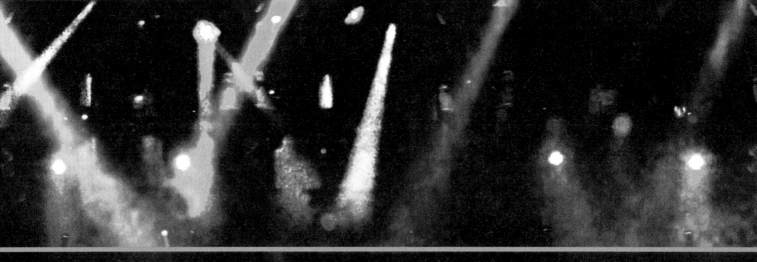

questioning. During his appearance on the show in November 2011, David joked about Justin's new 'Believe' tattoo on his arm while Justin responded by calling David "Grandpa". JB went on to perform his new single 'Boyfriend'.

The X Factor USA

Justin joined the finalists of The X Factor USA during a star-packed final show last year. JB showed that he's more than just an incredible performer when he turned mentor to contestant Drew Ryniewicz and invited her onstage to perform with him and music legend Stevie Wonder.

CSI: Crime Scene Investigation

Justin surprised the TV critics and fans alike with a mature and impressive performance in his first full acting role. JB played troubled teen Jason McCann on the crime drama – an angry young man who had been brought up in a series of foster homes prior to being adopted. When his adopted father is arrested, Jason swears revenge on the police. Justin's natural, subtle performance was a huge hit and after two appearances on CSI he left fans and critics looking forward to his next dramatic turn.

LIGHTS, CAMERA, BELIEVE!

Justin Bieber – Never Say Never

JB made his big screen debut in a documentary charting the ten days leading up to his 31st August 2010 concert at Madison Square Garden in New York. The movie features rehearsal footage, bags of live performances and interviews with a host of Justin's family, friends and fellow celebrities, but none with the man himself.

The centerpiece of the film, the huge concert, was one of the first times a live performance had been captured in full 3D. Naturally JB didn't disappoint. As well as performing his own popping-out-of-the-screen versions of his greatest hits, Justin was joined onstage by Usher, Ludacris, Miley Cyrus and Boyz II Men.

More than just a concert movie, Never Say Never also told the inspiring story of Justin's rise to fame. It showed JB's belief that we're all in charge of our own destiny. "I wanted to let people know there's a lot of people that are discouraging in life and that will tell you you can't do something, but you just got

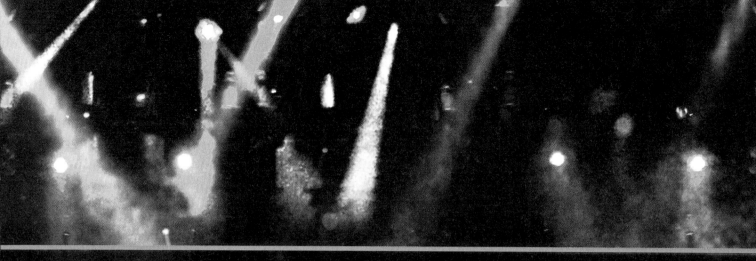

o remember that the sky's the limit," Justin explained. "You're able to do whatever you set your mind to as long as you remember to keep God first and stay grounded. So I think the movie really explains that, and it's really inspiring."

Even by Justin's own high standards, the film was huge smash hit around the world. Industry insiders say the film cost $13million to make (a small budget for a major movie) but earned an incredible $98.5million at the box office.

In the process Justin had become not only a bankable movie star, but also an award-winning one. The film won the 2011 Best Jaw Dropping Moment at the 2011 MTV Movie awards!

Despite becoming a star in a new field, Justin was quick to share Never Say Never's success with his Beliebers. When attending the film's premières around the world, JB made sure he took the time to thank as many of his fans personally as he could!

FACT OR FICTION?

No matter what he does, Justi
can't help being a consta
source of rumour and gossi
Rarely a day goes by without
story appearing in newspape
columns, celebrity website
or trending on Twitter. Wit
so much JB talk out ther
real Beliebers need to be ab
to separate the true storie
from the fakes. Read the 1
statements below. Can yo
sort out the genuine Just
from the bogus Biebers

2. Bieber is huge football fan, having trained with both Barcelona and Chelsea players.

Fact ☐   Fiction ☐

1. For a short while in 2010 Justin was engaged to reality TV star Kim Kardashian.

Fact ☐   Fiction ☐

3.Lots of people think Justin's middle name is Drew. It's not. It's actually Drewley.

Fact ☐   Fiction ☐

4. Record executive Scooter Braun discovered JB in 2008 after spotting him on YouTube.

Fact ☐   Fiction ☐

5. Although he spends most of his time in America, Canadian Justin has often said he has no interest in obtaining US citizenship.

Fact ☐   Fiction ☐

6. Justin's mum Pammie can often be seen by his side at award shows.

Fact ☐   Fiction ☐

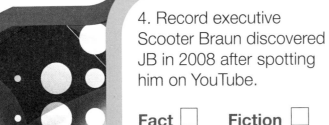

7. Justin dated fellow Disney names Miley Cyrus and Demi Lovato before settling on Wizards of Waverly Place star Selena Gomez.

Fact ☐   Fiction ☐

8. JB was on a short tour with Taylor Swift when he broke his leg on stage.

Fact ☐   Fiction ☐

9. One of the first things Usher did when he started working with JB was to ask his assistant Ryan Good to work with Justin as a stylist.

Fact ☐   Fiction ☐

10. Justin rented the entire 20,000 seat Staples Center in Los Angeles to have a candle-lit dinner with Selena in 2011.

Fact ☐   Fiction ☐

11. JB very nearly didn't become the pop star we know today as he was once offered the chance to play professional ice hockey for the Toronto Blue Jays.

Fact ☐   Fiction ☐

12. Justin Bieber – Never Say Never 3D was originally planned to be the first music film released in 4D, but the extra dimension proved too expensive.

Fact ☐   Fiction ☐

13. Since recording his first album, Justin has had to lower the keys of some of his biggest hits as he can no longer hit the high notes!

Fact ☐   Fiction ☐

14. Justin called in an eclectic mix of musicians to help him when recording his new album 'Believe', including Jay-Z, Metallica and Jedward.

Fact ☐   Fiction ☐

15. By having his haircut in 2010, Justin cost Bieber product manufacturers over $100,000!

Fact ☐
Fiction ☐

JUSTIN BIEBER

WELCOME TO THE BIGTIME!

Scooter Braun had earned a reputation around Atlanta as one of the city's finest promoters. When big acts passed through the area, it was Scooter they turned to organise them the best parties. But even as his career took off, his ambition and drive wouldn't let him rest, he wanted something more.

In the summer of 2007, he found it while browsing online. Scooter stumbled across a video of Justin singing R&B songs at home in one of Pattie's YouTube clips. He instantly recognised Justin's potential and knew that if he could get this young Canadian kid to work with some of the contacts he'd built up, he had a shot at the big time.

After a lot of hard work, Scooter managed to track Pattie down. However, for a while, she wouldn't take his calls. Eventually he got through, although Pattie says she called him back simply to tell him to stop calling her! In a two-hour conversation Scooter persuaded Justin's mum to visit him in Atlanta.

When Pattie and Justin made it to Atlanta, Scooter backed up every promise he'd made on the phone. He introduced JB to Usher and vocal coach Mama Jan, as well as setting up an industry showcase at Eddie's Attic.

Realising he'd been given a once in a lifetime opportunity, Justin didn't disappoint on stage. Usher, who by now taken him under his wing, saw that JB was ready to take it to next level. He decided there and then to set up a company with Scooter and sign a record deal with Justin.

JB's time had come…

"Justin is truly talented. He is that special superstar that you see once in a lifetime. He plays four instruments, self-taught. He showed that in his YouTube channel. He had an incredible tone in his voice. He was captivating." Scooter Braun

"When I met him, his personality won me over. When he sang, I realized we were dealing with the real thing." Usher

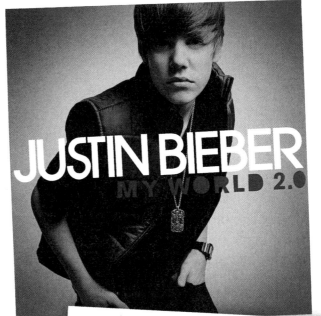

JUSTIN BIEBER
MY WORLD 2.0

TEAM

BIEBER

Now you're Justin's VIP guest! Read on and enjoy exclusive access to the entourage that surrounds our star.

Pattie Mallette

Justin's mum Pattie, brought Justin up single-handedly after she split from his dad, Jeremy. Today, she's still most-likely to be found at Justin's side despite becoming something of a celebrity in her own right. Although their life has come along way from those early days in Stratford, Pattie's the one that keeps Justin grounded 24/7.

Scooter Braun

Record executive Scooter was the guy who discovered Justin Bieber. While trawling for new talent on YouTube in 2008, Scooter stumbled across a video of JB singing and was instantly hooked. Braun has managed Justin ever since and the pair enjoy a close friendship as well as being business partners. Type 'With You - Chris Brown Cover - Justin singing' into YouTube and check out the video that first caught Scooter's eye.

Usher

No points for guessing who the first celebrity Belieber was! R&B star Usher was one of the first to recognise Justin's star potential and has been a constant mentor and friend to JB ever since. When he needs some support, advice or simply a few wise words from someone who knows the business inside out, Usher is the person Justin calls.

Ryan Butler and Chaz Somers

Justin's oldest friends are fellow Stratford kids Ryan and Chaz. The trio met at elementary school and can often be found messing around together backstage at JB concerts. But despite being super-proud of his best friend's fame and success, Ryan has admitted he still misses his pal. "I'm really proud that he put himself out there and was found, out of millions of people," Butler explained. "Still, I miss him and feel sad he hasn't been able to play sports like other kids and do the usual kid stuff."

Mama Jan

Everyone who's anyone has worked with vocal coach Jan Smith, better known as Mama Jan. Justin puts the strength of his singing voice and the fact he's been able to make it through recording four albums and a 130 date world tour to the lessons that Mama Jan has taught him.

Ryan Good

Justin calls Ryan his 'swagger coach'! The pair worked together on all of his signature looks and more recently Ryan worked with JB as an art director on the album packaging and photo shoot for 'Believe'. The pair are, often swapping quips on Twitter.

Selena Gomez

Before going public with their relationship at the 2011 Oscars® in Los Angeles, there were many rumours that JB and Selena were an item. The couple are now regularly snapped together and seem as into each as they ever have been. Despite regular stories that they are planning to get married however, both insist that they are happy just having a good time!

Taylor Swift

One of Justin's best friends is country star Taylor Swift. JB calls her 'the sweetest girl ever', but that didn't stop him playing a prank on her when he made a guest appearance on the MTV show Punk'd. Biebz persuaded Taylor that she had accidentally blown up a boat loaded with fireworks for the show. Luckily it didn't take Taylor long to forgive Justin – she appears on a track on his new album.

Barack Obama

When Justin performed at the White House in December 2011 he got to spend some time with the American President. With two teenage daughters, it's no shock that Obama knew all about JB, but after meeting JB the President admitted that he was a fan too.

Kim Kardashian

Reality TV star Kim was one of the first celebrities to admit she had been struck down with Bieber fever. Kim revealed her feelings in a series of tweets that made many think the pair were actually an item. Both Justin and a smitten Kim later explained that they were just good friends!

Timbaland

Justin struck up a close friendship with super-producer Timbaland when the pair worked together on Justin's album 'Believe'. Timbaland's a good friend to have in the music business. After producing tracks for everyone from Justin Timberlake and Keri Hilson to Madonna and Jay-Z, he's one of the most connected people in the industry.

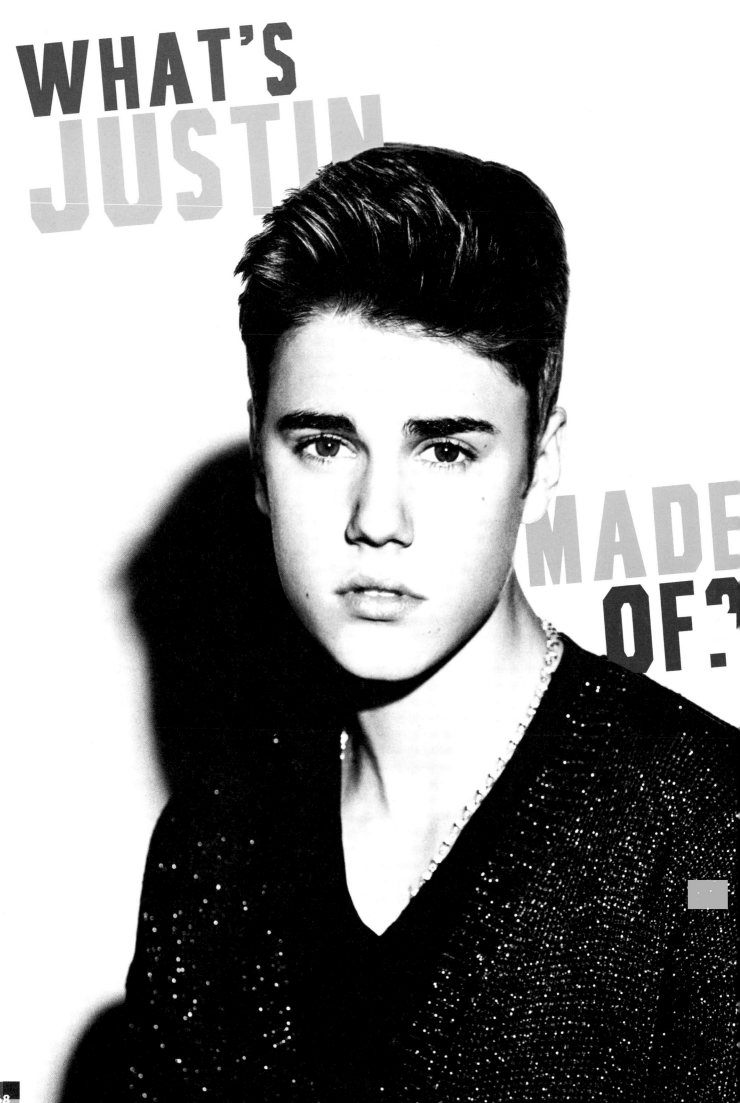

WHAT'S
JUSTIN

MADE
OF?

These days, you need a whole host of different skills to make it in the world of music, and even more to sustain a career. Being a great singer or a skilled dancer alone just isn't enough! We think we've worked out the heady mix of ingredients that make JB such a star. Have we missing anything? Write your theory at the bottom of the page.

Belief – As Justin explained in his film Never Say Never, throughout his life he has always proved his doubters wrong. While others didn't think he could make it in one of the toughest industries in the world, Justin has always believed in himself. The sky's the limit as far as this star goes!

Individualism – Justin is truly one of a kind. Even in his early days in the music business he has always done things his own way. Whether that's being brave enough to step outside his field and act on TV (as he did in CSI), re-record one of his songs in a completely different musical style (check out his country-tinged version of 'That Should Be Me' with Rascal Flatts) or take a chance on a new artist (as he did with Carly Rae Jepson), Justin follows his heart and does things few other artists would try.

Excitement – With his choices, many talents and passion, Justin has made music exciting again. From the first time he appeared on record, music fans were psyched to discover a talented new artist bringing out a whole new sound. The first time we all heard 'Boyfriend', any doubts as to whether he could follow up the success of his last album disintegrated immediately. In short, JB is one of the most thrilling artists in the world!

Bravery – Justin isn't afraid to take risks. Throughout his career he has consistently put himself in positions that would terrify most other musicians. He regularly challenges his talent by working with the very best names in the business, continues to try his hand at a variety of different musical styles, exposes himself and his true feelings by writing his own songs and steps out of his comfort zone to experiment in different fields.

Energy – While the rewards for being a pop star are high, the work it takes to become one should never be underestimated. JB is a tireless worker on all aspects of his career. Every show gets 100% and each vocal in the studio is given the maximum effort. Justin gives hundreds of interviews and appears on masses of TV and radio shows, always flashing his winning smile. And when the star is not working, he's interacting with fans online. Justin has energy to burn!

Rhythm –Justin plays four different musical instruments and never misses a beat whether singing or dancing. While there's no doubt that JB has a huge natural talent, he's not afraid to rehearse, rehearse and rehearse again to get each number step perfect.

I think Justin is something special because ....

....

....

....

WALLS & WHEELS

Growing up in Stratford with his mother has invested Justin with a humble attitude towards money and the trappings of fame. However, with the guidance of manager Scooter and mum Pattie, JB has made his first steps onto the property ladder. He's also been lucky enough to indulge in his passion for cars.

"I don't love money, because once you start loving money, you've got a big house and nice cars and just an empty heart, and that's the truth, I'm not just saying that. I've got my eye on a few things to spend my money on. I've got my own bank card, but I am really good with money. I don't spend too much at all."

Hometown Stratford

Justin's home in Canada has become a tourist spot for Beliebers, with fans visiting the small town for a look at the house Justin grew up in. The local residents and council are rightly proud of their famous son. They have even produced a handy printed guide called the Bieber-iffic Map To Stratford!

JB's Atlanta digs

Justin's home in Georgia is situated in an ultra-exclusive area of Atlanta, known as Buckhead. Bieber alumni including Usher, Lil John and Ludacris all live close by so JB's never short for neighbours to visit if he runs out of sugar!

California king bed

In March 2012, it was reported that JB had bought a luxurious $6million home in Calabasas, California. The property is said to have six bedrooms, seven bathrooms, six fireplaces, two separate garages, an elevator, a pool and spa, and a detached casita. Wow!

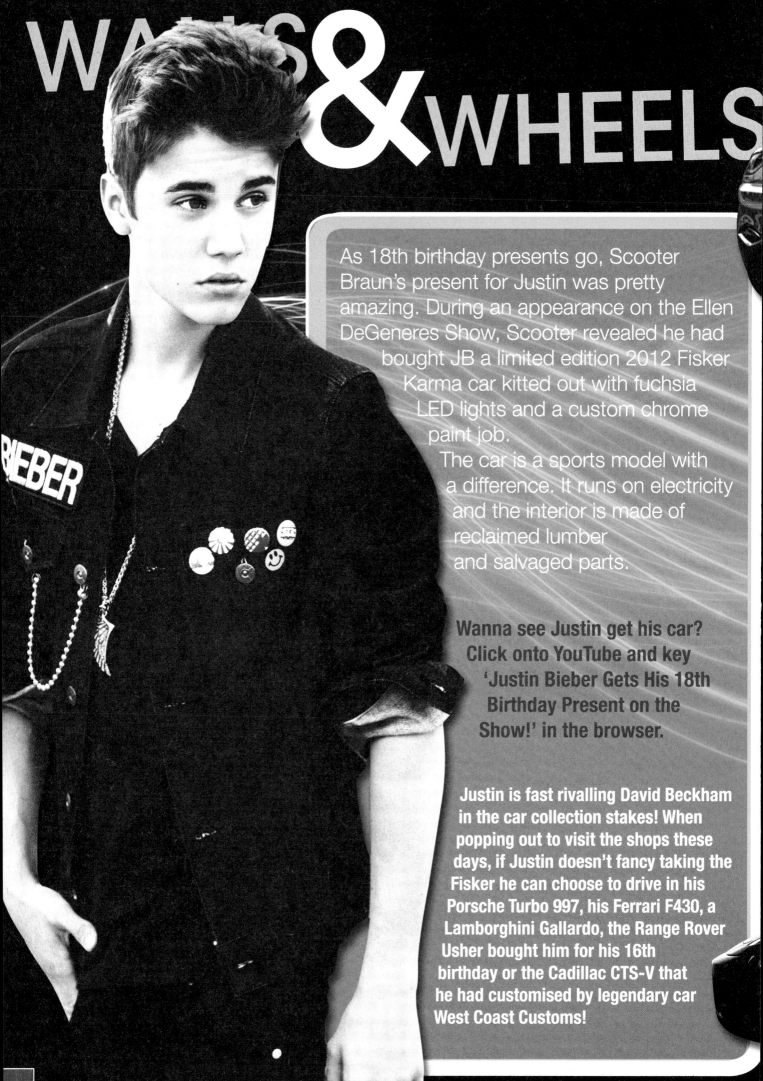

WALLS &WHEELS

As 18th birthday presents go, Scooter Braun's present for Justin was pretty amazing. During an appearance on the Ellen DeGeneres Show, Scooter revealed he had bought JB a limited edition 2012 Fisker Karma car kitted out with fuchsia LED lights and a custom chrome paint job.

The car is a sports model with a difference. It runs on electricity and the interior is made of reclaimed lumber and salvaged parts.

Wanna see Justin get his car? Click onto YouTube and key 'Justin Bieber Gets His 18th Birthday Present on the Show!' in the browser.

Justin is fast rivalling David Beckham in the car collection stakes! When popping out to visit the shops these days, if Justin doesn't fancy taking the Fisker he can choose to drive in his Porsche Turbo 997, his Ferrari F430, a Lamborghini Gallardo, the Range Rover Usher bought him for his 16th birthday or the Cadillac CTS-V that he had customised by legendary car West Coast Customs!

Range Rover

Fisker
Karma

Cadillac CTS-V

Ferrari F430

CRAZY CROSSWORD

These crossword questions are not as easy as you'd think! For a real challenge, have a showdown with a Bieber-loving pals to see who can crack the most clues in under two minutes! Ready to be challenged? Bring it!

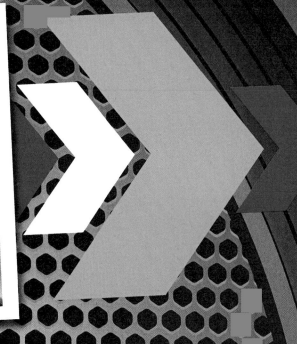

Across

2 The place where Justin was born. (6)
4 Selena Gomez aside, the celebrity singer Justin admits to having a crush on. (7)
5 The single JB released in March 2010. (1, 5)
8 Fans of Justin are said to suffer from a condition known as Bieber _ _ _ _ _. (5)
9 The rap superstar that remixed the track 'Runaway'. (5)
10 JB's star sign. (6)
12 The instrument that Justin straps on to perform 'Favourite Girl' on tour. (6)
14 The symbol Justin has tattooed on his elbow? (4)

Down

1 The city that Justin currently lives in? (6)
3 The track that Jaden Smith joined Biebz to rap on. (5, 3, 5)
6 A hit JB lyric that goes, 'Shawty is an _ _ _ _ _ _ _ _ _ _ _ mo lover.' (5, 6)
7 Justin's nickname for his tour entourage. (8)
11 The pasta Justin likes to eat best with Bolognese sauce. (9, 9)
13 The name Justin's fans are known as? (9)
15 The surname of Justin's manager Scooter. (5)

JUSTIN
BY NUMBERS

Have you got JB's number? Here are just a few of the icons most important digits…

2
Justin opened up for Taylor Swift at two concerts on her UK tour in 2009. During the first night he broke his leg, but he didn't let that stop him performing for the fans the next evening!

4
Justin's age when he got his first drum kit.

The number of tracks from Justin's debut album, 'My World 2.0', to appear in America's Billboard Hot 100 chart – a world record. **7**

2
Justin appeared in two episodes of the cop show CSI: Crime Scene Investigation's eleventh series. JB played troubled Jason McCann on the show, breaking hearts when his character was dramatically killed off.

13
The number of music videos Justin has made to date.

18
Despite spending two years touring the world as a professional musician, JB only officially became an adult on 1st March 2012.

During his short career, JB has won 67 awards including four AMAs, six Billboard awards and one BRIT. **67**

20,000,0000+

JB's ever-increasing number of Twitter followers – more than Justin Timberlake and Eminem put together, and second only to the most followed person on Twitter, Lady Gaga.

24,000

The number of Twitter followers JB gains on average every day!

The zip code for Buckhead, Atlanta – the exclusive town where Justin now lives.

30305

47,500

The largest audience Justin played to when his 'My World' tour stopped in Mexico city.

1,000,000

JB's videos passed the 1billion views mark You-Tube in November 2011, just ahead Gaga! How long before he hits a trillion?

130

The number of concerts on Justin's 'My World' tour.

The number of albums Justin has sold to date.

JUSTIN BIEBER ON THE ROAD

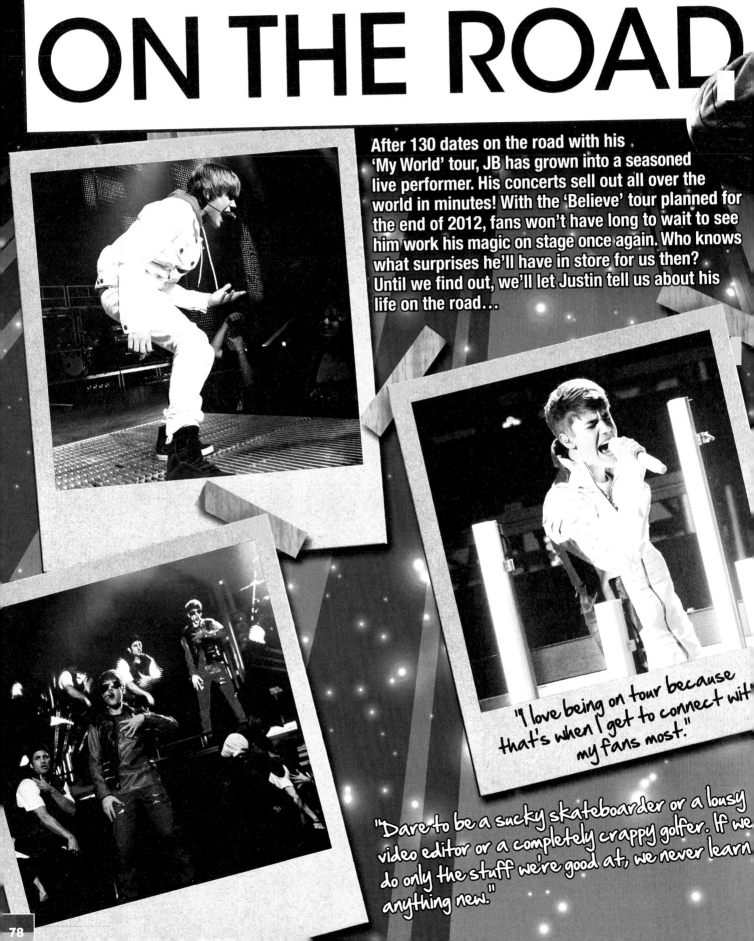

After 130 dates on the road with his 'My World' tour, JB has grown into a seasoned live performer. His concerts sell out all over the world in minutes! With the 'Believe' tour planned for the end of 2012, fans won't have long to wait to see him work his magic on stage once again. Who knows what surprises he'll have in store for us then? Until we find out, we'll let Justin tell us about his life on the road…

"I love being on tour because that's when I get to connect with my fans most."

"Dare to be a sucky skateboarder or a lousy video editor or a completely crappy golfer. If we do only the stuff we're good at, we never learn anything new."

"...just being able to be on tour ...avel the world has been the best part of it."

"The Beliebers have done some pretty crazy stuff. Last week, the night before I was due to do a show in Germany, four girls went into a dumpster so they could sneak into the building. They climbed in and hid!"

JUSTIN BIEBER
ON THE ROAD

"Singers aren't supposed to have dairy before a show, but we all know I'm a rule breaker. Pizza is just so good!"

"I've had a few gigs where things have got out of hand and there has been a huge crush with my fans. They are important and I don't want them being hurt. They are a mad crowd."

'Down To Earth' is a huge fan favorite. So many people feel where I'm coming from. It doesn't need any spectacular stage effects in the touring show; the best thing I can do is just sing it straight from my heart. I'm not afraid to show my emotions; if you love someone, you should tell them. If you think a girl is beautiful, you should say that."

"I think that it's important that people see this and see my story because it gives people hope."

There's gonna be times in your life when people say you can't do something. And there's gonna be times in your life when people say you that you can't live your dreams. And there's gonna be times in your life when people say you that you can't sell out Madison Square Garden! This is what I tell them: Never say never!"

JUSTIN BIEBER

JUSTIN THEN, NOW & FOREVER

After signing with Scooter and Usher, Justin was soon working on his first album. When he relocated to Atlanta he was also getting his first taste of being a star. JB's YouTube following was reaching insane levels and, as his reputation spread, fans were starting to ask when his music was going to be released.

When Justin hit the studio, Usher ensured that top songwriters and producers were around to work on the record. He even called in some of his friends to appear on the album too. By early 2009, JB's first single was ready to released. 'One Time' charted highly around the world and whetted fans' appetite for more.

JB was a unique type of performer. He could sing and dance, he looked great and a queue of respected artists wanted to work with him, but despite all the fame and success, he would still interact directly with people on social media. No other star combined such talent with such a humble attitude. The fans were crazy about him.

After releasing several singles and an EP in 2009, Justin finally dropped his first album the following year. Preceded by 'Baby', 'My World 2.0' saw JB not only hit the big time, but truly become one of the

biggest artists in the world. His huge world tour, smash hit movie and TV appearances only further proved it.

Mr Bieber has truly arrived on a global scale. With a new album and second world tour under his belt, the Justin phenomenon can only get bigger!

"I believe in myself, dreams, that I can do anything. I believe in so many things. I think that word is so powerful and I want to inspire everybody to believe."

"Travelling the world. I'd never been on a plane before all this happened ☺ I have the fans to thank for that."

JB ON LOVE

Justin has mentioned in several interviews that he is a true gentleman who likes to keep his private life out of the press. However, while not being one to kiss and tell, over the years the hottie has revealed some of his thoughts on dating and love…

JB on the day his life changed forever…

"Nothing ever got my pulse racing (in a good way) like hockey. Well, nothing except Beyoncé, but that wasn't until I was twelve or so. Then, all of a sudden, it was like I opened my eyes one day and noticed that the world is full of beautiful girls, and I've had a hard time thinking about anything else ever since!"

Justin on knowing his limitations…

"I have crushes, but they're all too old. Like Beyoncé, she has a husband, I might get shot! I went up to give Beyoncé a hug at the Grammys and Jay-Z said, 'watch out buddy!' He was kidding, but you know!"

JB reveals what it takes to catch his eye…

"A girl has to have a beautiful smile, beautiful eyes and she should have a good sense of humor. She should be honest, loving and trustworthy."

Justin's ideal woman is…

"Cheryl Cole and Katy Perry are two of the hottest girls in the world – and so normal and funny with it. If I was a few years older they are the kind of girls I'd like to date. I want a younger version of Cheryl and Katy – a mixture of the two would be hot. I would like to invite the two of them out for dinner so they can tell me the best way to win a woman like them!"

For JB, it's all in the chemistry…

"I hate being on a date where both people are working too hard to come up with stuff to say. You know it's working when you can just chill – listen to music, watch a movie, or whatever. It would be a shame to go out with a hot girl you can't have a decent conversation with."

"Not trying to be arrogant, but if I walked down the street and a girl saw me, she might take a look back because maybe I'm good-looking, right?"

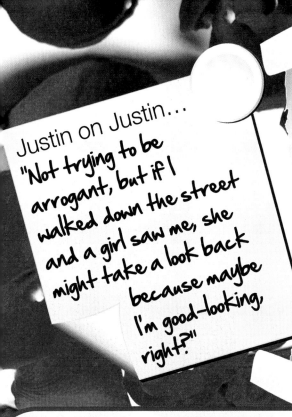

FYI, Justin Bieber is fluent in love…
"Now I'm really glad that I speak French, because, let's face it, girls dig it when a guy speaks French. They call it the language of love, and that ain't no coincidence!"

JB tells Ellen what attracted him to Selena Gomez… **"She has very kissable cheeks."**

Justin lays bare the realities of a celebrity relationship… **"I mean, for me, it's like, there's no way to hide it completely, because then it would be** unfair for us. Then, we're not even able to have a relationship. It's like, 'You take this car, and I'll take this car, and then we'll meet up at the spot. Then, you go in this door, I'll go in this door. We'll end up crossing ways. You get back in this car. We'll cross over, do a James Bond. You go through the kitchen. I'll go through the back area. Then we'll meet in the dressing room and see each other.' At that point, it's like, it's not even a relationship. You're just hiding from everyone. That's unfair and unhealthy, man."

JB's future love dreams…
"True love is so important. If someone found true love while listening to 'Boyfriend',

WILD WORDSEARCH

1. Justin's Christmas-themed album was called '_ _ _ _ _   _ _ _
_ _ _ _ _ _ _ _'.

2. The first single from Biebz' third album debuted to a huge fanfare in
March 2012. It is titled '_ _ _ _ _ _ _ _ _'.

3. Justin is proud to call _ _ _ _ _ _ home.

4. JB duetted on 'Never Say Never' with another teen idol, _ _ _ _ _ Smith.

5. Justin's first album and world tour shared the same name – '_ _ _ _ _ _ _'.

6. 'Baby' is the Biebz's biggest hit to date, but he didn't sing it alone. He
pulled in rapper _ _ _ _ _ _ _ _ to help him out.

7. Of course, Justin isn't just an incredible musician, he can act too! He won
huge praise for his role in _ _ _ _ _ _ _ _ _ _ _ Investigation.

8. The world got wise to Justin's talents the moment he released his first
single, the simply brilliant '_ _ _ _ _ _ _'.

9. Justin's mum _ _ _ _ _ _ _ _ _ _ _ _ _ is a constant companion and
source of advice for JB whether he's at home, in the studio or out on the road.

10. Justin set a huge record in July 2010 when the video for his track
'_ _ _ _' became the most viewed in YouTube's history.

11. Justin's girlfriend _ _ _ _ _ _ Gomez is a superstar in her own right,
famous for her hilarious Disney show The Wizards of Waverly Place.

12. JB is a box office smash. His first film, Justin Bieber – _ _ _ _ _ _ _ _
_ _ _ _ made an incredible $30.3million in its first weekend alone!

13. Throughout his career, Justin has been mentored by R&B superstar _ _ _
_ _ _ _ _ _ _ _ _.

14. JB's second single, 'One Less _ _ _ _ _ _ _ _ _ _', was a smash hit all
over the world.

15. While out on tour with country star _ _ _ _ _ _ Swift, Justin sustained a
broken foot.

16. Sean Kingston joined Justin on the catchier-than-a- cold hit '_ _ _ _ _
_ _ _ _ _'.

17. JB rose to fame when his manager _ _ _ _ _ _ Braun accidentally
clicked on one of Justin's homemade YouTube videos.

18. _ _ _ _ _ _ _ is the title of Justin's long-awaited new album

By now, you should be totally tuned in to everything Bieber. But can you fill in the brainteasing gaps opposite, then find where each answer is hiding within Justin's wickedly hard wordsearch? The words on the grid could be running in horizontally, vertically, diagonally or even back to front! Get your pens at the ready…

B	O	Y	F	R	I	E	N	D	B	G	G	S	V	A	D	A	N	A	C
F	B	N	N	F	D	S	H	U	K	L	P	T	Q	V	N	W	T	K	R
U	E	E	V	J	S	L	U	D	A	C	R	I	S	R	P	I	O	M	I
N	Q	A	Z	W	A	S	C	R	F	Y	H	N	S	B	A	B	Y	V	M
D	P	K	H	Y	F	D	R	W	B	Q	A	C	H	K	T	S	W	Y	E
E	G	A	L	D	L	J	E	W	O	E	H	O	N	E	T	I	M	E	S
R	E	R	O	R	D	C	V	N	Q	A	F	S	A	E	I	G	L	K	C
T	E	T	O	T	W	N	Q	E	R	G	T	Y	S	T	E	T	R	P	E
H	F	W	Q	S	L	E	P	R	D	U	W	P	B	U	M	D	W	Y	N
E	Y	U	L	C	E	V	H	Q	Q	S	E	L	E	N	A	G	V	W	E
M	H	Y	O	T	R	E	T	P	Y	H	G	E	L	R	L	E	P	F	Y
I	A	W	N	B	W	R	E	Z	I	E	L	G	I	W	L	Q	J	C	V
S	S	Q	E	I	Y	S	W	Z	A	R	X	L	E	P	E	H	B	Q	E
T	Y	A	L	M	T	A	Y	L	O	R	Q	M	V	R	T	D	O	S	Q
L	J	J	Y	O	P	Y	G	O	E	A	E	B	E	I	T	B	N	C	J
E	K	P	G	N	E	N	Q	T	W	Y	Q	A	S	T	E	P	I	O	F
T	L	E	I	Y	Q	E	U	E	Q	M	P	L	M	C	A	I	K	O	P
O	S	Q	R	C	H	V	P	R	O	O	D	P	D	Q	H	C	G	T	W
E	C	C	L	W	L	E	D	E	E	N	I	E	M	E	E	N	I	E	E
Q	W	B	M	A	S	R	B	P	H	D	A	F	G	H	Y	P	W	R	X

OUT OF THE SPOTLIGHT

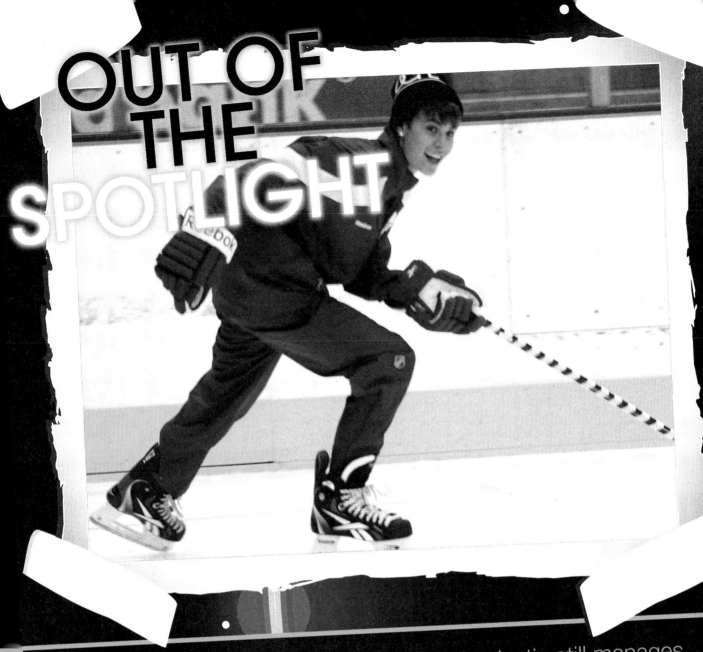

Despite being totally committed to his music, Justin still manages to find time to kick back and chill out…

• JB is a huge fan of ice hockey and his favourite team are the Toronto Blue Jays. When he can the star likes to take to the ice and hit a few slap shots.

• It's not just hockey either, Justin is a total sports addict who loves to stay active. While out on the road, he jumped at the chance to train with the Chelsea first team and enjoy a kickabout with the football legends at Barcelona.

• Justin also spends tons of time on his skateboard. When taking a break from recording 'Believe', Justin tweeted his followers to let them know that he was skating at a friend's house. The friend in question happened to be rap superstar and fellow skater, Lil Wayne.

• Growing up in Stratford, Justin didn't have many chances to see the world outside of his small Canadian town. The star has made up for that now and enjoys the odd day off from his tours to explore new cities.

• As well as catching up with his family, Justin likes nothing better than heading back home to hang out with his best friends Ryan Butler and Chaz Somers. With a job that means he's always the centre of attention with every move he makes is being scrutinized, JB relishes the chance to shrug off his airs and graces and chillax.

WHATS
NEXT?

Much as we'd like to, none of us, not even Justin, can tell what the future holds. But that doesn't stop it being fun to try! What will you be doing in five years time? What will Justin's life look like in ten years? Obviously, you'll still be a Belieber, but what differences will there be between now and then? Fill these pages with your future predictions, keep this annual safe, then check back in years to come and see if you were right!

In five years time I will be

By that point, Justin Bieber will have

The biggest fashion will be

The latest gadget that everyone will be playing with will be the

The most popular style of music will be

JBiebz will have started collaborating on tunes with

But the biggest change in my life will be

In ten years' time, the 29-year-old JB will be

I will be …… years old by then and will be

I will be living in

Despite all these changes, one thing is certain –
I'll still be running a Bieber fever!

JUSTIN BIE
ANSWERS

Page 18-19 Strictly Lyrics
1 Buzz LightYear
2 after the song
3 butterflies in my stomach
4 We're just friends
5 that drives me
6 start overs
7 time to sink or swim,
8 thousand miles
9 of my dinner
10 to run across the sea
11 Reindeers flying
12 sucker for love
13 doubters on
14 waiting so long
15 will stand
16 kept my heart
17 to Be Loved
18 baby baby baby
19 be homeless
20 fight the feeling

Pages 32-33 Tricky Titles
1 Stuck In The Moment
2 Overboard
3 Up
4 That Should Be Me
5 Down To Earth
6 First Dance
7 Bigger
8 Live My Life
9 Kiss And Tell
10 Born To Be Somebody
11 Rich Girl
12 Fa La La
13 Next 2 You

14 Home This Christmas
15 All I Want Is You
16 All Around The World
17 Die In Your Arms
18 As Long As You Love Me
19 Thought Of You
20 Be Alright

Pages 42-45 Step Up To…
The 2013 Bieber Quiz
1 'My World'
2 'One Time'
3 Jaxon and Jazmyn
4 Trumpet
5 March
6 19million
7 The Wolfpack
8 Three
9 Eddie's Attic
10 Ludacris
11 Willow Smith
12 He went busking
13 Scooter Braun
14 'Runaway'
15 Miley Cyrus
16 He sang the Usher classic 'With You'
17 Justin Timberlake
18 Justin Bieber – Never Say Never 3D
19 Michael Jackson
20 Mike Posner
21 Kid Rauhl
22 Usher
23 Four years old
24 Watertown
25 Bruce and Diane Dale

ANNUAL

Pages 60-61 Fact Or Fiction?

1 Fiction – Justin's never been engaged, although Kim Kardashian is a big fan.
2 Fact – during his 'My World' tour JB dropped in on both clubs.
3 Fiction – Drewley? Really!?
4 Fact – Scooter still manages Justin's career today.
5 Fact – Justin says Canada is the best country in the world.
6 Fiction – Justin's mum Pattie can often be seen by his side!
7 Fiction – Selena's the only girl for JB.
8 Fact – Justin was opening an arena show in London for Taylor when the accident happened.
9 Fact –Justin calls Ryan his 'swagger coach'.
10 Fact – romantic Justin was inspired by a scene in the Adam Sandler film Mr Deeds.
11 Fiction – Although he's a major ice hockey fan, JB has never been offered the chance to play professionally.
12 Fiction – three dimensions of JBiebz is enough for anyone!
13 Fact – Justin explained recently that his voice has got deeper in the last few years, 'like any teenage boy'.
14 Fiction – JB's actually been working with Timbaland, Lil Wayne and Kanye West.
15 Fact – Biebz's 2010 haircut has earned the reputation as being the most expensive of all time!

Pages 74-75 Crazy Crossword

Pages 86-87 Wild Wordsearch

1 'UNDER THE MISTLETOE'
2 'BOYFRIEND'
3 CANADA
4 JADEN
5 MY WORLD
6 LUDACRIS
7 CRIME SCENE
8 'ONE TIME'
9 PATTIE MALLETTE
10 'BABY'
11 SELENA
12 NEVER SAY NEVER
13 USHER RAYMOND
14 'LONELY GIRL'
15.TAYLOR
16 'EENIE MEENIE'
17 SCOOTER
18.'BELIEVE'